AWESOME COLORING BOOK for BOYS

Buckle up, kids! Time to dive into a
world of color and adventure!

From roaring engines to galactic quests,
every page promises a new thrill.
Let your imagination run wild!

Rolling Rides

Vroom! Vroom! Hop into the world of land vehicles, where speed meets the road. From the roaring engines of race cars to the determined chug of a tractor, this section celebrates everything that rolls and races. Ready, set, color!

Sports Car

Excavator

Sports Bike

Bullet Train

Dump Truck

Road Roller

4x4

Bulldozer

Vintage Cruiser

Super ATV

Classic Car

Classic Tow Truck

Tractor

Vintage Car

Sky & Sea Voyages

Soar through the skies and dive into the deepest oceans with our collection of air and sea vehicles. Feel the thrill of jet planes zipping through clouds or the majesty of ships cutting through waves. Let your imagination fly or swim as you color these amazing vehicles.

Cruise Ship

Fighter Jet

Regional Airliner

Jumbo Jet

Submarine

Chopper

Icons & Idols

Meet the heroes, legends, and the stars of the stage! Whether they're scoring a goal, playing a tune, or mastering martial arts, these figures are sure to inspire. Dive into the world of athleticism, music, and fantasy characters, capturing their essence with every color you choose.

Samurai Warrior

Ninja

Bass Player

Baseball Athlete

Skateboarding

Boy Band

Wilderness Explorer

Taekwondoin

Football Star

Soccer Player

Game Character

Slam Dunk

Fauna & Legends

Roar, growl, and howl! Welcome to a
world where wild beasts roam and
mythical creatures soar. Whether
it's a ferocious lion, a mythical
unicorn, or a towering T-Rex, embark
on a coloring adventure that brings
these creatures to vibrant life.

Which ones are real and
which ones are not? Can you guess?

Dragon

Great White Shark

Lion

Iguana

Sphinx

Goblin

Yeti

Eagle

T-Rex

Cosmic Quests

3...2...1... Blast off! Journey to the stars and beyond in this section dedicated to space adventures. Colorful rockets, mysterious planets, and maybe even an alien or two await. Get ready to explore the infinite wonders of the cosmos.

Alien

Satellite

Space Ship

Astronaut

Space Jet

UFO a.k.a. UAP

Tech & Hobbies

Step into the future and revisit the past with this eclectic mix of technology, gear, and cherished items. From sleek robots and musical instruments to vintage cameras and speedy F1 cars, there's a treasure trove of items waiting for your artistic touch.

Game Controller

Space Jet

Space Jet

Electric Guitar

Mountain Biking

SLR Camera

Kicks

Formula 1

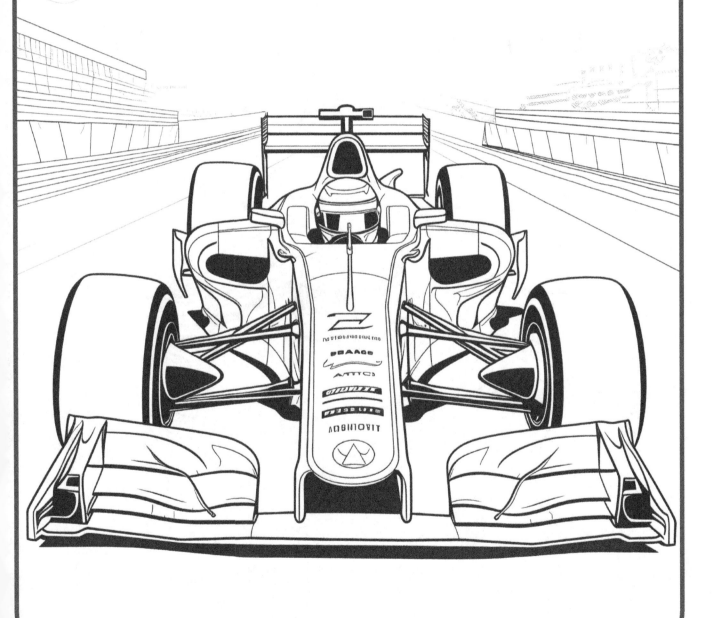

Drone

Tree House

Majestic Realms

Discover the hidden corners of the world, both real and imagined. Majestic mountain peaks, awe-inspiring wonders, and secret dwellings like tree houses and spooky mansions all await your colors. Dive in and let your creativity shape these magical landscapes.

Yosemitet

The Great Wall

Haunted House

Active Volcano

Ancient Ruins

Colosseum

Egyptian Pyramid

Greek Temple

Congratulations, young artist!
You've brought life to every page with
your vibrant colors and imagination.

This certificate is a testament to your hard
work and artistic spirit. Well done!

This certificate is awarded to:

Thank you for joining us on this colorful journey! We hope your little artist had a blast. If you enjoyed the adventure, we'd be grateful for a review on Amazon.

Your feedback helps us create more delightful experiences!

Made in United States
Orlando, FL
20 December 2023

41517621R00043